SCRUM ART
HAND BOOK

SCRUM ART
HAND BOOK
SCRUM TOOL BOOK

DURGA MADIRAJU

Copyright © 2018 by Durga Madiraju.

ISBN: Softcover   978-1-5434-7416-9
           eBook   978-1-5434-7415-2

All rights reserved. No part of this book may be reproduced or transmitted in any form or by any means, electronic or mechanical, including photocopying, recording, or by any information storage and retrieval system, without permission in writing from the copyright owner.

Any people depicted in stock imagery provided by Thinkstock are models, and such images are being used for illustrative purposes only.
Certain stock imagery © Thinkstock.

Print information available on the last page.

US Copyright for Business Improvement Model

Rev. date: 01/18/2018

To order additional copies of this book, contact:
Xlibris
1-888-795-4274
www.Xlibris.com
Orders@Xlibris.com
771789

CONTENTS

Foreword ix

Chapter 1   Scrum Overview 1
Chapter 2   Scrum Facts 2
Chapter 3   Scrum Experiences 3
Chapter 4   Scrum Tool Requirements Pyramid 5
Chapter 5   Scrum – Deliver the Three what's 6
Chapter 6   Scrum – Iteration Readiness Checklist 7
Chapter 7   Effective Scrum Master Tips 8
Chapter 8   Scrum User Story Dependency Fulfillment 9
Chapter 9   Scrum – Template Driven Emails 11
Chapter 10   Scrum Daily Standup-Call Readiness 13
Chapter 11   Scrum: User Story Task breakdown 14
Chapter 12   Iteration – Team Member Progress Checklist (Tool) 15
Chapter 13   Scrum Master: Iteration Completion Checklist 16
Chapter 14   User Story Acceptance fulfillment Checklist 17
Chapter 15   Release Package Readiness 18

SCRUM ENHANCEMENTS/IMPROVEMENTS
PART 2

Chapter 16   Iteration Shortcomings 23
Chapter 17   Scrum Performance Improvements 24
Chapter 18   Scrum Note 25

Chapter 19 User Story Utilization Categories and value added factors 26
Chapter 20 Scrum Release Crux – Decision points 28
Chapter 21 Use Case Scenarios 29
Chapter 22 Scrum marginal utilization theory 31
Chapter 23 Capabilities Efficiency Model 32
Chapter 24 Capacity Utilization Efficiency Computation 35
Chapter 25 Capabilities Efficiency Model: Case Analysis 40
Chapter 26 How to Bridge Product Requirements Gap 43
Chapter 27 Product Model Example: Open Continuous Model:... 44

SCRUM REPORTING
PART 3

Chapter 28 Purpose of Scrum Reporting 49
Chapter 29 Iteration Score Card Metrics 50
Chapter 30 Scrum Iteration – Best Scores 51
Chapter 31 Score Impact Card 52

APPENDIX SECTION

Appendix A Agile Model for Waterfall and Hybrid Agile Technologies. (An example) 55
Appendix B Sample Template for Daily Sprint Call 56
Appendix C Sample Template for Iteration Planning Session 57
Appendix D Template for Demonstration of User Stories 59
Appendix E Scrum Envelope: List of User Stories Ready 60
Appendix F USER STORY TEMPLATE (TOOL) 61
Appendix G Timetable for Demonstration of User Stories 62
Appendix H USER STORY COMPONENTS 63
Appendix I SCRUM SCRATCH PAD 64

Appendix J	Scrum Scratch Value	65
Appendix K	Scrum Scratch Content:	66
Appendix L	Scrum Chat Cubes	67
Appendix M	Scrum Scratch Pad Value Point Assignment	68
Appendix N	Scrum Scrub Pad Value	69
Appendix O	Scrum Scratch Note Example	70
Appendix P	User Story Completion Template Report	71
Appendix Q	Iteration Optimal Value Point	72
Appendix R	Scrum Daily Report Pad (Optional)	73
Appendix S	Scrum Release Time Table Example	74
Appendix T	Scrum Umbrella	75
Appendix U	Scrum Toolkit	76
Appendix V	Iteration Score Card Example	77
Appendix W	Marginal Utils Card	78

FOREWORD

Scrum in a nutshell, is a methodology, and a sub category of project management discipline. The processes discussed in different areas of project management discipline have been specialized and devised into a framework suitable for scrum.

Scrum Methodology leverages project management capabilities through accountability and responsibility with milestones defined in different phases of project life cycle. (Milestones are met through scrum ceremonies).

The scrum art handbook is a tool/guide to learn and manage scrum better. The scrum art handbook provides the reader with effective tips and techniques, and serves as a reference, to drive scrum for Agile.

A scrum master can use the tips defined in this book, to lead scrum teams with confidence, through a definitive approach. The book helps scrum teams to be scrum ready, and provides suggestions for improvements.

The book will help the scrum master take the next step forward, in not only developing and implementing efficient scrum processes but also in rethinking and retooling efficient practices and policies for effective scrum management.

The scrum art handbook, will help realize scaled agile practices for increased productivity and efficiency. The Lean and six sigma methodology techniques discussed in the capabilities efficiency model, and applied to portfolios, and release trains will help attain the goal of Scaled Agile Framework. The value added to, and marginal efficiencies derived from, through the capabilities efficiency model, is explained in the Capabilities Efficiency Model framework.

In short, the capabilities efficiency model identifies the shortcomings, (identified in the different categories of the project), and applies refactoring, and criteria revision, to bridge the deviation/variance between the base model and the revised model for improved productivity.

The base metrics and revised metrics serve as a guide in planning and reporting continuous iteration cycles and release trains (portfolios). The main goal of leveraging lean efficiencies is realized through optimization.

I would like to conclude with a brief note:

Scrum can be learnt and improved upon by fine tuning existing scrum processes, to come up with new theories and practices for maximum scrum utilization and optimization.

This book is only aimed at providing suggestions and remedial measures for effective scrum practices. The book does not deter or hinder or contradict any existing processes or methodologies, already in existence.

- *Durga Madiraju...*
  MBA, MS Information Systems, MA Economics
  Advanced Diploma in German
  Certified Scrum Master (CSM)
  Certified Six Sigma Green Belt and Lean Certified
  Quality by Design Certified
  Presidential Voluntary Service Award (2014-2016)

Member Voluntary Committees: AT&T
- WOA (Women of Atlanta) – Mentoring Committee
- APCA Judge (Asian Pacific Islanders for Professional and Community Advancement)
- Oxygen Mentor
- PAC (Political Action Committee) Ambassador
- OASIS Member
- Member of Technology Inventions and Process Improvements

Certificates and Awards at AT&T
- IT Wall of Stars
- IT professional Growth Award
- Technology Development Award
- Six Sigma Green Belt Growth Award

Publications:
- *Article publication: Agile, A Quality Metric Tool - Scrum Alliance*
- *Poems: Poems A Collection*
  - ***Seasonal Woods,*** *by Durga Madiraju as Jane Summers -* ***Vol 1***
  - ***Summer Woods,*** *by Durga Madiraju as Jane Summers -* ***Vol 2***

CHAPTER 1

SCRUM OVERVIEW

Scrum is an applied methodology of Agile Framework.
Another definition of Scrum is
"A methodology used to drive efficient utilization of resources and technology for iterative development of software in a time boxed cycle, through efficient use of tool."

Benefits leveraged from Agile Methodology:

- ✓ *Iteration completion with maximum utilization of user stories.*
- ✓ *Iteration completion with reuse of user stories.*
- ✓ *Avoidance of wastage of resources.*
- ✓ *Increase in marginal value derived from an iteration delivery.*
- ✓ *Techniques revised and improved, for better usage and implementation.*
- ✓ *Economies of scale obtained by delivering optimal number of user stories with minimal cost per iteration.*
- ✓ *Careful planning and refinement of user stories through a learning of Retrospectives.*
- ✓ *Optimal integration of user stories from UI and database end to avoid re-development cost.*

The benefits of scrum: It is easily adaptable and customizable.

CHAPTER 2

SCRUM FACTS

- ✓ Scrum is a different mentoring experience every day.
- ✓ Scrum is a different theme/highlight, learnt from a mentoring experience the previous day.
- ✓ Scrum is a repository of facts based on learning from a previous iteration.
- ✓ Scrum is the foundation, we build upon based on key takeaways of learning of an iteration.
- ✓ Scrum can be customized to suit company situations, circumstances, and events.
- ✓ Scrum is fine-tuned and better adapted overtime.

Just the Facts

CHAPTER 3

SCRUM EXPERIENCES

Scrum is a different experience for a scrum master, and is a value measure of iterations. Scrum experience varies based on size of company, application and technology, but the basic tenets of scrum remain the same.

Scrum by industry size
A small and mid-sized company may have scrum teams that maybe smaller in size where the Role of a scrum master may overlap several roles. A scrum master may be a developer, a tester, and an architect etc.

A large company may have an agile framework, which is a hybrid of waterfall and Agile. A scrum master's role in a large size company is simplified with team members and architects specialized in their roles, performing their job duties and responsibilities with minimal effort.

No matter what type of agile framework a company adopts, each phase in the development cycle of Agile methodology, will include the following functions:

- ✓ *Scrum Teams responsible from development phase through implementation phase and post support phase of Agile iteration cycles.*
- ✓ *Scrum Team(s) overlap of Roles in: Development, Test, Defect, Release, and maintenance phase categories.*

- ✓ *Scrum Teams trained in expertise and commitment to continuous delivery of software.*
- ✓ *Scrum teams Process of simplifying work when encountering issues in the course of development.*

Please refer to Appendix A for an example of Waterfall, and Hybrid Agile Implementation.

CHAPTER 4

SCRUM TOOL REQUIREMENTS PYRAMID

Advanced Layer Fulfillment
User Story Creation
Task Creation
Task Fulfillment
Demo Fulfillment
User Story Completion
User Story Acceptance

Intermediate Layer Fulfillment
Release Backlog Plan
Sprint Backlog Plan
Product Backlog Plan
Standardized Query for User Story view

Base Layer Fulfillment
Team Access of Tool
Capacity Estimates

Note: The tool referred to in this page is for example purposes only. The tool used to manage scrum process varies by company.

CHAPTER 5

SCRUM – DELIVER THE THREE WHAT'S

- ✓ *Answer the 3 what's*
  - What have you worked on yesterday?
  - What are you working on today?
  - Are there any impediments/issues in user story progress?
- ✓ *Progress the 3 what's.*
- ✓ *Deliver the 3 what's.*
- ✓ *What's = Goal Fully Met = Iteration complete.*

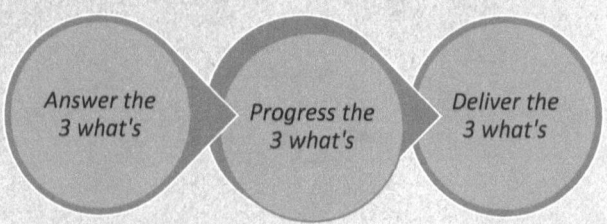

CHAPTER 6

SCRUM – ITERATION READINESS CHECKLIST

- ✓ *Plan and verify capacity estimates of current iteration.*
- ✓ *Verify inclusion of wire frames/html/design/technical solution documents in the acceptance criteria for a user story.*
- ✓ *Verify story point assignment of a user story.*
- ✓ *Verify match in time and availability of team members and business architects during requirements/architecture/demonstration/acceptance phase of user stories.*
- ✓ *Verify environment readiness (to develop and test) of user stories.*
- ✓ *Verify Release Date of user stories.*
- ✓ *List user stories for delivery in the iteration.*
- ✓ *Verify user story assignment of team members.*
- ✓ *List integration user stories ready for delivery.*
- ✓ *Verify cut-off date for addition of a user story in an iteration.*

CHAPTER 7

EFFECTIVE SCRUM MASTER TIPS

Effective scrum practices, help bridge scrum gap for optimal results and delivery.

- *Read and Review chapters on iteration preparedness, meeting readiness, status update readiness and work completion requirements.*
- *Communicate using a well prepared Agenda.*
- *Reach out to participants, the expectations and techniques of goal attainment in scrum ceremonies.*
- *Keep Communication Bridge open (to facilitate quick resolution) for successful completion of an iteration.*
- *Send communique with regards to offshore holidays and leave of absence for smooth work transition.*
- *Use of the word "We", "We need to deliver", "We need to resolve blockers/issues", "we need to be prepared", "Team" in scrum meetings will help scrum teams build confidence and support.*

Scrum Ethics: *PCR*

- *P - Perseverance*
- *C - Commitment to deliver*
- *R - Reliance/Dependence*

CHAPTER 8

SCRUM USER STORY DEPENDENCY FULFILLMENT

A dependent user story, to meet the criteria of "fulfilled", needs to meet the criteria checklist listed below.

Criteria Checklist Summary:
Organize, sequence, and complete a user story dependency, for automation to help fulfill the criteria of 'User Story dependency met'.

Steps for criteria fulfillment are listed below:

- ✓ Categorize and group dependent user stories together.
- ✓ Validate criteria check for completion of a parent user story.
    - o Validate and verify Requirements completion.
    - o Validate and verify development and test Environment readiness.
    - o Validate and verify Test case scenario completion.
    - o Validate and verify Resource assignment.
    - o Validate and verify data availability.
- ✓ Schedule a dependent user story, with the following criteria:
    - ✓ Estimate time required to complete parent and child user stories.
    - ✓ Simulate a prototype, to ensure all use case scenarios have been validated and tagged for success (both parent and child user stories).
    - ✓ Schedule the release date, of parent and child user stories based on the dependencies fulfilled.

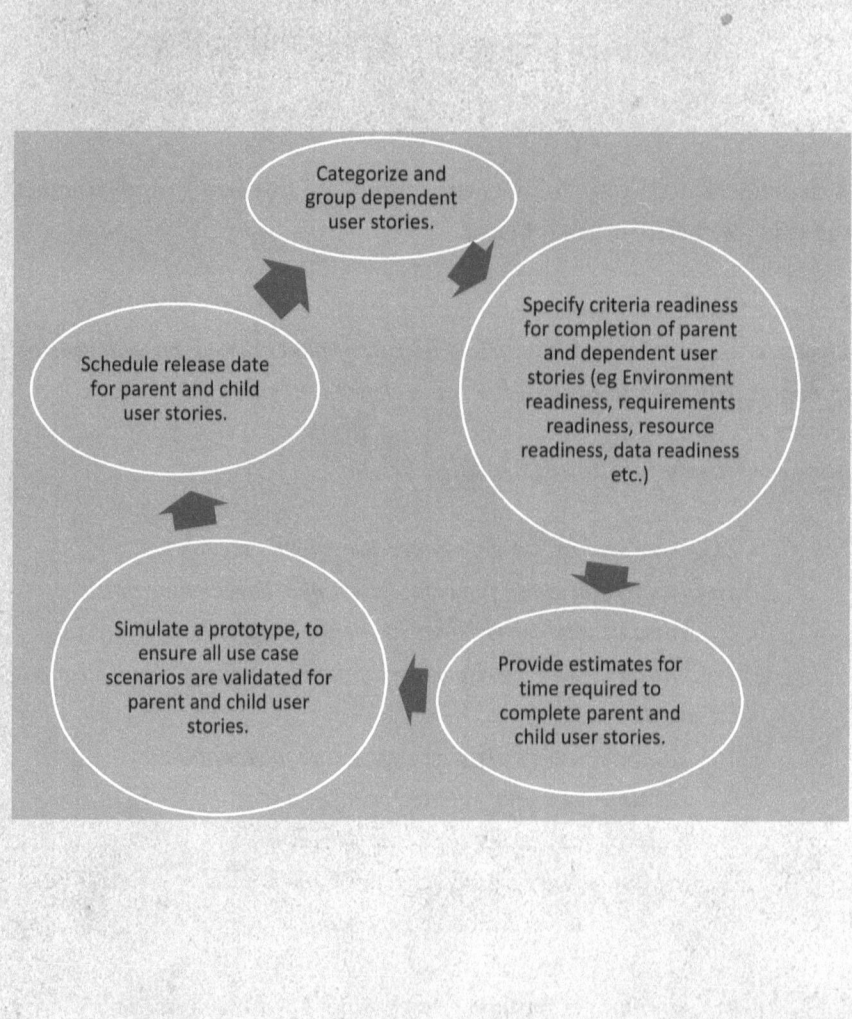

CHAPTER 9

SCRUM – TEMPLATE DRIVEN EMAILS

Template driven emails increase process efficiency and productivity. Agendas emphasize scrum values, and drive expectations for better results.

Please see appendix section for examples of email templates:

Appendix B: A template driven email for Iteration Planning sets expectations for the following:

- ✓ User story readiness.
- ✓ User story organization and simplification.
- ✓ User story dependency fulfillment.
- ✓ User story creation fulfillment.

Appendix C: A template driven email for daily sprint call highlights procedures for iteration fulfillment.

- ✓ Use of Guidelines for adherence towards completion.
- ✓ Receive questions and provide answers on time.
- ✓ Automate task phases.
- ✓ Automate handoff for smooth transition.
- ✓ Automate goals for delivery on time.
- ✓ Automate status updates.

Appendix D: A template driven email for Demonstration of user stories, sets expectations for the following:

- ✓ *Automate solution demonstration.*
- ✓ *Automate verification and validation for completion.*
- ✓ *Automate user story acceptance for approval and tagging.*
- ✓ *Automate audit compliance, and on time.*

CHAPTER 10

SCRUM DAILY STANDUP-CALL READINESS

Team Readiness:

- ✓ On-Time Daily Attendance.
- ✓ Prompt daily status updates.
- ✓ Progressive task status updates.
- ✓ Smooth resolution of issues:
    - User story blockers
    - User story dependency solution(s).
    - Environment solution(s).
    - Data Readiness/Availability solution(s).
- ✓ Schedule adherence for various milestones.
- ✓ Responsibility and accountability for fulfilling criteria of self-organized.
- ✓ Smooth transition of tasks for successful completion.

CHAPTER 11

SCRUM: USER STORY TASK BREAKDOWN

The following is a breakdown of tasks in scrum tool.

- ✓ *Code/Development.*
- ✓ *Unit Testing.*
- ✓ *Code Review.*
- ✓ *Validation.*
- ✓ *Demonstration of User Stories.*
- ✓ *Proof of Verification/Completion with screenshots.*
- ✓ *Acceptance by Technical Architect/Business Architect.*

CHAPTER 12

ITERATION – TEAM MEMBER PROGRESS CHECKLIST (TOOL)

Daily Progress Check: Team Member:

- ✓ *Set task status to In-Progress.*
- ✓ *Strikethrough/update a task when a task is complete. (Tool used is a scrum Tool)*
- ✓ *Schedule Demonstration of user stories with team members and Business Architects.*
- ✓ *Set child user story to a status of complete.*
- ✓ *Tag all tasks to approved.*

CHAPTER 13

SCRUM MASTER: ITERATION COMPLETION CHECKLIST

- ✓ Set user stories to a status of complete, when all tasks are complete.
- ✓ Move user stories to a new iteration, not completed in the current iteration.
- ✓ Add closing comments to a user story after a user story has been accepted.
- ✓ Tag user stories to a status of approved.
- ✓ Verify that user stories have been balanced across all scenarios, before moving to the next iteration.

CHAPTER 14

USER STORY ACCEPTANCE FULFILLMENT CHECKLIST

Acceptance must meet the following criteria:

- ✓ *Accepted = Accepted at the iteration level (code complete, test complete, validation complete, integration complete, Demo complete, accepted by Architect).*
- ✓ *Accepted = Accepted at Stakeholder Review Meeting.*
- ✓ *Accepted = Release Deployed successfully and approved by the client.*
- ✓ *Accepted = Feature Applied and Used – Approved by the client.*
- ✓ *Accepted = Tagged and Approved in the system, for Audit and Compliance.*

CHAPTER 15

RELEASE PACKAGE READINESS

Iteration Release Readiness:

All user stories identified as 'Ready' and committed to an iteration are targeted to a Release. The following factors influence release readiness and need to be verified for Release.

- ✓ *User stories committed to a Release.*
- ✓ *Project Resource Availability.*
- ✓ *Project Manager Availability.*
- ✓ *Project Release Date.*
- ✓ *Release Communication Template Readiness.*
- ✓ *Release Gaps*

Release Gap Identification

- ➤ *Project Factors committed to, and not ready to meet target release date:*
    - ○ *Environment failures.*
    - ○ *Data failures.*
    - ○ *Release Manager Availability.*
    - ○ *Deployment Failures.*
    - ○ *Other failures.*

> *Identify failures in deliverables broken down by:*

Code and Test failures broken down by the following categories:
- *Verify code review of user stories for success/fail*
- *Verify integration test cases for success/failure*
- *Verify Regression test cases for success/failure*

Release Readiness Measures: Applied to code, test, deployment, environment, program management etc.
- *Bridge the gap of failure scenarios by validating the flow through the capabilities efficiency model, and also for reuse.*
- *(Walk through failure scenarios using question/answer approach for analysis and resolution).*
- *Implement revised measures by category, and regenerate success cases.*
- *Compute metrics of the revised measures implemented.*
- *Reuse continuous revised measures for iteration cycles.*

> *Identify failures in a Releases by readiness, availability, poor resource management, and other categories*
> *Compute/compile measurable value of the failure scenarios to re-evaluate the impact of an iteration in relation to previous iterations. Assign success/failure rules to different categories of business improvement rules.*
> *Tag business rules for approval and audit.*

Agile Release Communication

Release communication is defined as a formal/informal communication by a project manager for delivery of software in increments, on a date/time agreed upon.

Agile Release Commitment
Release Commitment criteria is defined as: Meets criteria of deliverables agreed upon with Release Date committed.

Release Commitment Criteria = Deliverables Agreed upon + Release Date Committed.

Agile Release Ready
Release Ready = Approved and Tagged Ready for Release.

SCRUM ENHANCEMENTS/ IMPROVEMENTS

PART 2

CHAPTER 16

ITERATION SHORTCOMINGS

User Stories not completed for various reasons are listed below:

- *User stories transitioning to a different path, not meeting the criteria of "done."*
- *Tech spikes/defects, moving into a different estimation and date of completion, losing track of the original estimation, and falling behind in feature completion.*
- *Duplication and Poor Definition "of user stories".*
- *Procedures not defined for resolution and recurrence of failures.*
- *User Stories not meeting the definition of acceptance criteria.*
- *User stories de-scoped in the current iteration, and not back tracked for proper scoping.*
- *User stories not addressed for lack of effective policy planning.*
- *Improper scheduling of user stories*
- *Lack of definition of dependent user stories.*
- *Work incomplete on a user story, of tasks not complete, when the iteration ended.*
- *User stories not in compliance of the auditing process.*
- *Completed user stories not audited on time.*

CHAPTER 17

SCRUM PERFORMANCE IMPROVEMENTS

Scrum performance improvements for improved productivity are listed below:

- ✓ Hold Parallel scrums for different categories such as feature sets, environment readiness, Data Readiness, for efficiencies.
- ✓ Sequence user stories for marginal efficiencies.
- ✓ Synchronize user stories for Parallel Release to reap benefits of economies.
- ✓ Organize user stories awaiting defect fixes for release efficiency.
- ✓ Identify and reutilize user stories for value.
- ✓ Determine scope through a process, using the capabilities efficiency model.
- ✓ Reorganize product backlog user stories through use case scenarios.
- ✓ Prototype test case scenarios, to avoid requirements gap, so that user stories are made iteration ready.
- ✓ Implement case template approach mentioned in the capabilities efficiency model for success/failure scenarios.
- ✓ Map user stories to an iteration only after the dependent user stories are complete.
- ✓ Resize user stories to smallest unit for delivery and value, so that they can easily be addressed, without blockers.
- ✓ Adherence to time-table to improve demonstration schedule will help avoid mismatch in time and availability of resources.
- ✓ Automate capabilities efficiency model.

CHAPTER 18

SCRUM NOTE

A scrum note may be defined as "an improvement to rethink a resolution or an issue for a resolution. A scrum note for a project can serve as a guideline for improvement(s).

A scrum note for simplicity, can be broken down into 2 parts:

- ✓ A note for a project can be an issue or a problem that needs to be resolved.
- ✓ A note for a project can be an improvement that was identified in the iteration.

Please refer to Appendix G for an example of a Scrum Note

Pick a note/comment that needs resolution/improvement in the scrum call		notes become the Retrospectives		notes serve as a guideline for improvement in Agile Progression

CHAPTER 19

USER STORY UTILIZATION CATEGORIES AND VALUE ADDED FACTORS

The following is a list of value added factors that serve as a guideline for effective user story utilization

- ✓ *Custom integration of user stories for optimization.*
- ✓ *Fine Tuned User Stories for value.*
- ✓ *Marginal Value derived from user story utilization.*

User Story utilization can be derived from the following categories:

- ✓ *Requirements Utilization Category*
  - ✓ *Requirements common across features identified for use/reuse.*
  - ✓ *Requirements for enhancements mapped to standard use and custom use.*
  - ✓ *Requirements refined/re-defined for proper utilization.*
  - ✓ *Requirements balancing all scenarios.*
- ✓ *Code Utilization Category*
  - ✓ *Identify and prepare code failure and code success scenarios.*
  - ✓ *Group reasons and categories for code failure and code success scenarios.*
  - ✓ *Provide solutions for success. Reuse solutions for similar cases in different iterations.*
  - ✓ *Identify maximum code utilization across all scenarios.*
  - ✓ *Tag and approve all code failure and code success scenarios.*

- *Defect Utilization Category*
    - *Identify and prepare use case defects.*
    - *Requirements identification, and defect use cases need to go hand in hand.*
    - *Prepare use case scenarios remedial measures.*
    - *Provide solutions for success/failures of defect scenarios.*
    - *Tag and approve all failure and success scenarios.*
- *Release Utilization Category*
    - *Identify Release Failures.*
    - *Provide categories with detail to walk through scenarios of Release failures.*
    - *Provide Controls and measures for release readiness, so that Release failures do not recur.*
    - *Please refer to Release Package Readiness chapter for release readiness measures.*
    - *Tag and approve all release success and failure scenarios.*
- *Other Categories*
    - *Bridge gap to identify failures in all the above categories.*
    - *Map use case scenarios with remedial measures and add to the list of remedial measures.*
    - *Implement remedial measures in test environment.*
    - *Standardize measures across all features, and for reuse.*
    - *Tag and approve balanced cases with success and failure scenarios.*

CHAPTER 20

SCRUM RELEASE CRUX – DECISION POINTS

Decisions Influencing User Story Release:

- ✓ On-time defect resolution constraints.
- ✓ On-time design Implementation constraints.
- ✓ Environment constraints.
- ✓ Access constraints.
- ✓ Decision crux points evaluation.
    - ✓ Does the user story meet the feature set defined in requirements? Complete the checklist, using the question and answer model approach.
    - ✓ Is the iteration deployment ready? Complete the deployment checklist, using the question and answer model approach.
    - ✓ Has the release criteria readiness checklist been met? Complete the checklist, using the question and answer model approach? Please refer to chapter on Release Package Readiness.
    - ✓ Is the crux impacting scenarios balanced across all scenarios? Please checklist the scenarios, as approved and tagged.

CHAPTER 21

USE CASE SCENARIOS

Wrong Scenario Example(s):

a. Code usage scenarios to be documented for understanding.
b. Code changes completed, but code changes need to be revised as it did not meet product requirements?
c. Code changes need to be revisited at a later point in time, as the scope is incomplete.
d. Shipped Features implemented but require revision.
e. Child stories need to be revised and relinked to the parent epics.
f. Code validation needs to be readdressed.
g. User story failures need to be documented for further improvement.
h. Test cases have not addressed all scenarios.

Right Scenarios:
 a. Defect categorization and organization for simplification
 b. Feature set categorization for easy user story definition.
 c. Feature set organization for indexing.
 d. Feature set indexing for reporting purposes.

Please refer to capabilities efficiency model for more detail:

 a. Code complex scenarios simplification.
 b. Code impact scenarios simplification.
 c. Code validation scenario simplification.
 d. Defect categorization and organization
 e. Defect grouping and tagging for backtracking and reporting purposes.
 f. Feature set categorization simplification.
 g. Feature set organization by user story for completion.

CHAPTER 22

SCRUM MARGINAL UTILIZATION THEORY

Marginal Utilization Theory Definition: Additional value derived from not only realizing product value, but also adding additional value to product. (Scrum product Realization).

From customer point of view, Marginal Utilization Theory implies adding additional value to consumer utils, resulting in increased consumer utilization. (Please refer to measure of utils scale).

Marginal Utilization theory aims at adding additional value to

- ✓ *Existing capacity resources.*
- ✓ *Optimal utilization through user story efficiencies.*
- ✓ *User Story utilization/reutilization.*
- ✓ *Progressive iteration through incremental value.*
- ✓ *Effective and efficient scrum delivery.*

Benefits derived from Marginal Utility Theory:

- ✓ *Utilization of user stories is optimal.*
- ✓ *Product Value realized is optimal and maximized*
- ✓ *Marginal value added is > 0 per iteration.*
- ✓ *No negative value: Zero Defects is one example case.*

Validity of Marginal Utilization Theory can be proved through iteration score metrics. Empirical studies derived from score metrics can be linked to capabilities efficiency model for usage.

CHAPTER 23

CAPABILITIES EFFICIENCY MODEL

Valued added categories for reutilization are listed below and can be verified using the Capabilities Efficiency Model:

- ✓ Requirements Re-utilization Category (s).
- ✓ Design/Code Re-utilization Category (s).
- ✓ Defect Re-utilization Category (s).
- ✓ Release Re-utilization Category (s).
- ✓ Other Category (s).

Category	Subcategory	Analysis	Implementation
Re-evaluation (Problem Analysis)	Re-evaluated list Sub-category(s)	Reference: chapter 25: Improvement Scenarios Re-evaluated analysis.	Question/Answer.
Revised (Prototype)	Revised list Sub-category(s)	Reference: chapter 25: Improved Scenarios Revised Prototype.	Case scenarios. success/failure path Artificial intelligence checks for predicting outcomes. Regenerate data with metrics for reporting purposes. Compute base model using a variance of 0.001

Re-generated	Re-generated list of Sub-category(s)	Reference: chapter 25 Regenerated Data and metrics for reporting purposes.	Pass/Fail. Optimization.
Statistical Models applied for trends and observations	Create efficiency model for continuous improvement.	Create metrics for optimization models.	Score Card.

Capabilities Efficiency Model Description:
Use Case Template Approach
- ➤ Requirements Reutilization Category:
    - ○ Requirements for user stories already defined or new requirements will be put in a category for business rules improvement
    - ○ Requirements in the category will be reviewed for reuse/optimal use and serve as a baseline for planning and designing future studies.
    - ○ Revised Criteria will be generated and prototyped.
    - ○ Metrics will be computed and verified against the baseline for fulfillment of the capabilities efficiency model.
    - ○ Functional specification and Design document will be verified against, to ensure that the regenerated model meets the Capabilities efficiency model for design.
- ➤ Design/Code Reutilization Category:
    - ○ Please refer to Capabilities efficiency model in the previous table.
- ➤ Defect Reutilization Category:

- Defects addressed as well as any new defects need to use the Capabilities efficiency model.
  - Defect solution fixes for the application need to be studied and reviewed, and revised using the capabilities efficiency model.
  - Defect fixes using the capabilities efficiency model need to be accepted and tagged for approval.
  - All defects addressed using the capabilities efficiency model need to be verified against baseline metrics for reporting purposes.
- Release Reutilization Category:
  - Please refer to the Capabilities Efficiency Model in the previous table.
- Other categories need to be defined for use, and for revision and for new improvements, and innovations in the Capabilities efficiency model.

Capabilities Efficiency Optimal Value Formula:
Compare regenerated metrics against Capabilities Efficiency Model (baseline): to arrive at optimal value. Optimal value is defined below:
Meets capabilities efficiency optimal value point >= 95% per iteration
Meets marginal efficiency value point >= 1.0 point to arrive at additional value per iteration

CHAPTER 24

CAPACITY UTILIZATION EFFICIENCY COMPUTATION

Please refer to Appendix M. The worksheet shows calculated and compiled iteration metrics for an iteration completed:

- ✓ *Compare and use existing Iteration capacity estimates for future planning.*
- ✓ *Compare Product backlog user story estimates for future planning.*
- ✓ *Metrics of past iterations to be compared with current iteration metrics and applied for efficient usage and estimations.*

Steps for computing the metrics
Issues in the current iteration
Revised Criteria and Measures
Applied Measures
Compute Metrics after revision
Compare Base Model with Metrics
Check for Optimal Value

Steps for Computing the Capabilities Efficiency Model

Data Collection from Past Metrics
Data Categorization
As Is Value Stream - current
Root Cause analysis
Cause and Effect Diagram
Problem Clouds
FMEA Analysis
ANOVA
Do Phase
As is Value Stream Future
Ranking Matrix chart - pick chart
Prioritization of recommendations through Ranking Chart
Counter Measures
Check Phase
Compute Solution Effectivemess
Checklist Measures
Implement
-.xls attachment of Analysis of Project
Graphs showing root cause, trend analysis, Pareto and Radar charts
Adjust Phase
Control Measures
List Issues after Implementation

Issues Identified - Category	Description of Issue	Link to Issue
Requirements and Design Category		
Defect Category		
Release Category		
Other Categories		

Revised Criteria - Category	Description of Revised Criteria
Requirements and Design Category	
Defect Category	
Release Category	
Other Categories	

Example computation

Model Applied	Current Metrics	Revised Criteria Metrics
Iteration1		
Stories addressed	40	
Categories (for expansion)		
Requirements Failure	5	
Design/Code Failure	4	
Defects Failure	6	
Deployment Failures	3	
Release Failures	4	
	22	
Requirements Readdressed		3
Design/Code Readdressed		3
Defects Readdressed		3
Deployment Readdressed		2
Release Readdressed		2
Total		13
Data Collection Techniques		
Source: Data collected from iteration		
Data Analysis		
Quantitative Research		
Descriptive Statistics		
Compute Mean		
Compute Median		
Compute Mode		
Standar Deviation		
Statistical Techniques		
Covaraince		
Correlation		
ANOVA		
Regression Analysis		
Confidence Interval		
Test of significance goal		
Inferential Statistics		
Random Sampling		

Compare the variation over iterations with the base model

Variance	Base Model	variance

CHAPTER 25

CAPABILITIES EFFICIENCY MODEL: CASE ANALYSIS

Article: *Defines Problem Scenario:*
(Article: provides user story number, failure scenario of the user story.)
Example: Article no: 45367-> Error bringing up the wrong values in the dropdown: user story no 58765

Comprehension (Detail): *Provides analysis and solution* *(Answer to user story failure 344213 -> 45367)*

Analysis: *Identify the problem at hand using question/answer centered approach.*

Case Detail: *Provide answer scenarios using examples and a question and answer approach, problem elimination approach. Similar to artificial intelligence behavior. Please refer to the capabilities efficiency model.*

Result oriented approach linked to the following criteria:

- ✓ *A limitation impact for continuous integration cycle.*
- ✓ *Scope identification without product impact to fulfill price and customer base.*
- ✓ *Efficiencies identified to efficient usage, showing usage metrics.*
- ✓ *Identify product value based on criteria/category for a complete definition of product realization.*
- ✓ *Qualitative Case Analysis Approach.*
- ✓ *Collaborative case approach.*

- ✓ Resolution identification techniques.
- ✓ Conditional fulfillment: strengths vs weaknesses.
- ✓ Partial Fulfillment: strengths vs weaknesses.
- ✓ Containment of product for a limitation: strengths vs weaknesses.
- ✓ Scoping efficiencies – identification, pattern match, segmentation, and strategy listing
- ✓ Map the product value efficiencies to user story scenarios.
- ✓ Scope utilization approach is based on product value efficiencies.
- ✓ Simplify requirements/design for easy adaptability and use.

Scope Result Approach worksheet: (Attach a scope result worksheet)
Problem documentation with example scenarios.
Problem isolation with example scenarios.
Value identified scenarios run through a prototype.
Metrics of prototypes for scoping efficiencies.

End Note (Scoping Report): Arrive at comments/note with supportive facts and metrics.

Success and Failure Metrics Model:

- ➤ Measure occurrences of success/failures.
- ➤ Categorize success/failure scenarios.
- ➤ Assign a weighted value to success/failure cases and prioritize the list.
- ➤ Compute Statistical techniques through a Regression model. Determine the covariance, coefficients for a positive and negative impact of the success/failure scenarios.
- ➤ Metrics computed will help narrow down solution efficiencies, and come up with a capable efficiency model.
- ➤ Create the capable efficiency model with past and current data, current and projection estimates for purpose of comparison and future planning.

Category	Subcategory	Analysis	Process
Re-evaluated category	Re-evaluated list of Sub-category(ies)	Reference: chapter 25 Improvement Scenario Re-evaluated criteria applied.	Question/Answer.
Revised category	Revised list of Sub-category(ies)	Reference: chapter 25 Improvement Scenario Revised criteria applied.	Checklist (Verification).
Re-generated criteria	Re-generated list of Sub-category(s)	Reference: chapter 25 Improvement Scenario Regenerated criteria applied.	Pass/Fail.
Statistical Techniques applied for trends and observations	Create efficient goal metrics	Create metrics for pass/failures.	Score Card.

CHAPTER 26

HOW TO BRIDGE PRODUCT REQUIREMENTS GAP

Product Requirements Gap Model:

Process Identification to bridge requirements gap:

- ✓ *Define/Identify parameters in a process.*
- ✓ *List the parameters that increase efficiency by order of ranking.*
- ✓ *Plug the parameters (defined as factors) that will increase efficiency, as a weighted measure for each product. (Supportive cases with metrics).*
- ✓ *Compute the metrics*
- ✓ *Highlight product efficiencies that can be achieved by listing scenarios/use cases.*
- ✓ *Assign weighted value to business rules.*
- ✓ *Identify wasted effort/inefficiencies under categories, using a weighted measure for each inefficiency.*
- ✓ *Define user stories based on the efficiencies of the product model.*
- ✓ *Define Re-use efficiencies under categories.*
- ✓ *Rewrite Re-utilized based criteria stories.*
- ✓ *Identify and list process efficiencies for each user story.*

Example of Product Requirements Gap

Example: Orders are placed through different interfaces into the system.
Failures in business rules in the business layer.
Fields defined not used properly in the database.

CHAPTER 27

PRODUCT MODEL EXAMPLE: OPEN CONTINUOUS MODEL:

Improvement Scenarios for thought:

- ✓ Reutilization of user stories identified and linked for efficient usage.
- ✓ Value assigned user stories identified (using a weighted measure (ranked)) for future planning.
- ✓ Revised requirements criteria approach identified for adhering to question answer approach.
- ✓ Scarcity of usage scenarios identified and applied for effectiveness.
- ✓ Please refer to the utils card to verify if additional value was realized through.
  - Minimal use of resources (cost, labor, and quality)
  - Cost factors categorized and used for optimal usage.
- ✓ Customer concurrence on shipped iteration has been identified as value-added.
- ✓ Conditional fulfillment criteria has been identified and an example defined for implementation purposes.
- ✓ Partial fulfillment impact and effect on feature set has been identified and an example defined for implementation purposes.
- ✓ Rule definition criteria has been defined for the business processes, as a feature set.
- ✓ Scope failure definition has been identified and defined with example scenarios to backtrack for reference.
- ✓ Rethink scenarios of continuous integration cycle increments for optimal value.

How to measure value?

An example of scope definition by assigning yes/no, to criteria defined using categories bucket and a question/answer approach:

- Pass for success scenarios.
- Pass for negative scenarios.
- Fail for scenarios for past failures.
- Success for success scenarios.
- Define by example for all scenarios implemented in the iteration, both success and failure.

A few examples:

- ✓ A failure scenario, of a feature shipped (question/answer)
- ✓ A success scenario, of a feature being used (question/answer)

SCRUM REPORTING

PART 3

CHAPTER 28

PURPOSE OF SCRUM REPORTING

- ✓ *Metrics help assess requirements for user stories, help estimate optimal load in a sprint, help predict iteration fluctuations, and identify improvements for effective implementation.*
- ✓ *Metrics can be used for product enhancement studies.*
- ✓ *Metrics can be used as a guideline for Research and Development.*
- ✓ *Metrics can be used to improve the quality of workmanship.*
  - ○ *Metrics serve as a measure for assigning weightage to categories for ranking purposes:*
  - ○ *Metrics help identify Lean project management techniques, to redefine processes for better usage.*
  - ○ *Metrics make estimation viable and unquestioned backed up with supportive facts.*
- ✓ *Metrics can be used to measure quality assurance standards.*

CHAPTER 29

ITERATION SCORE CARD METRICS

What to look for at a quick glance in Iteration score card.

- ✓ Number of user stories delivered/shipped per iteration.
- ✓ Number of stories readdressed
- ✓ Number of user stories moved to next iteration.
- ✓ Number of defects addressed in the iteration.
- ✓ Iteration metrics
  - ✓ Team Capacity (Number of resources * hours * days) in the current iteration.
  - ✓ Velocity/Story points.
  - ✓ Burndown chart
  - ✓ Burnup chart

Compute the Three M's
- ➢ Mean
- ➢ Median
- ➢ Mode

Additional Metrics for computation
- ➢ Regression
- ➢ Correlation
- ➢ Covariance
- ➢ Radar spider charts

Please refer to Appendix V for score card

CHAPTER 30

SCRUM ITERATION – BEST SCORES

Scrum Value Point Measure (over 3 iterations)

- ✓ User Story Score Mean value over 3 iterations.
- ✓ Mode value: How many user stories were repeated over 3 iterations.
- ✓ Mode value: How many defects were readdressed over 3 iterations
- ✓ Iteration score variance for a 3 month period.
- ✓ Median Value over 3 iterations.
- ✓ Standard deviation.
- ✓ Variance.
- ✓ Correlation to measure the extent of correlation between two parameters identified in the model.

CHAPTER 31

SCORE IMPACT CARD

- ✓ *Identify, determine and compute the percentage impact of a user story failure.*
- ✓ *Categorize the impact by Code, Test, Requirements, Release criteria, or other factors.*
- ✓ *Compute the impact as a percentage of total user stories addressed in an iteration.*

Category	*Impact*
Code Failures	Impact by Code Failures %
Test Failures	Impact by Test Failures %
Scope limitation	Impact by Scope definition %
Release Failures	Iteration Impact failure = 10/30 *100 = 33.33%
Requirement Failures	Impact by Requirement Failures%

Define and list the impact by: Customer impact, Revenue/Loss, Resources.

- ✓ Code failure = 2 user stories
- ✓ Unit Test failure = 3 user stories
- ✓ Requirements failure = 2 user stories
- ✓ Release not met = 3 user stories

APPENDIX SECTION

APPENDIX A

AGILE MODEL FOR WATERFALL AND HYBRID AGILE TECHNOLOGIES. (AN EXAMPLE)

Traditional Waterfall	Hybrid Agile	Agile	Process	Ownership
BR (Business Requirements Specification)	BR (Business Requirements Specification)	BR (Business Requirements Specification)	PMO	PMO (Project Mangement Office)
Functional Specification	Epics/Sub Epics	Epics/Sub Epics	Systems Engineer	Tool
System Design	User story creation	User story creation	Technical Architect/Lead	Product Owner
Code/Unit Testing	Development/ Unit Testing	TDD – Test Driven Development	Sprint Planning Daily Stand-up Demo Retrospectives	Development Team
IST (Internal System Testing)	IST (Internal System Testing)	IST (Internal System Testing)	IST (Internal System Testing)	QA
UAT(User Acceptance Testing)	UAT(User Acceptance Testing)	UAT(User Acceptance Testing)	UAT(User Acceptance Testing)	QA
Production Release	Production Release	Production Release	Production Release	QA

APPENDIX B

SAMPLE TEMPLATE FOR DAILY SPRINT CALL

Agenda:

- ✓ What have you worked on yesterday?
- ✓ What are you working on today?
- ✓ Are there any impediments/issues/blocks holding up the user story?

Expectations:

- ✓ On time call attendance.
- ✓ Clarity in telephone and voice when communicating daily scrum updates.
- ✓ Inform team of offshore holidays.
- ✓ Inform if a team member is not able to take the call.
- ✓ Task Readiness of team members.
- ✓ Daily status update of tasks in the tool for progress monitor.
- ✓ Inform scrum master of any the following blockers/issues:
  - Blocking issues, a team member is waiting on such as requirements availability.
  - Dependency of a child user story on a parent user story.
  - Awaiting environment readiness.
  - Awaiting data readiness.
  - Not able to setup code reviews on time.
- ✓ Schedule demo timeline when the tasks have been given a timeline, with the team lead/BA?
- ✓ All Demos need to end 2 days before the iteration ends.

APPENDIX C

SAMPLE TEMPLATE FOR ITERATION PLANNING SESSION

Agenda:

Sprint Planning Session – Iteration No: mm/dd/yyyy – mm/dd/yyyy

User story Readiness in Tool: Product Owner

- ✓ Add Summary to the user story.
- ✓ Add Filed Against (OCE_ATG)
- ✓ Add Story size and **story points**
- ✓ Add Priority
- ✓ Add Owned by (Developer)
- ✓ Add Planned for (Release)
- ✓ Add Type of Impact
- ✓ Add description to the user stories
- ✓ Add acceptance criteria. Please see below (Definition of Ready) for acceptance criteria
- ✓ Add Related such as any other stories under the related section.
- ✓ Developer will break down the user story by tasks and estimate points and hours for task completion.

Other info for User Stories

- ✓ Add approvers under the approvers tab for every user story.
- ✓ Add any children/related info to the user story

Definition of Ready – Team D2

- ✓ User Stories -
    - ✓ Ensure US are identified as Mobile or Desktop.
    - ✓ Tag User stories with CMX, CMS, Content (CRD), Comps where applicable, Wireframes where applicable, HTML, Data Request, Design as completed.
    - ✓ Include Wire, comp, design, CMS XML, CMX, HTML, CRD links in the user story so they can be reviewed during sprint planning of that user story.
    - ✓ Dependent User Story Simplification and Organization.
        - User Acceptance Criteria (100% complete)
        - Mobile and Desktop HTML (incl. CSS and all images in SVN, End State HTML, HTML review)
        - Wires
        - Design Artifacts (External Dependencies like API calls)
        - Content Matrix (CMX) Update
            - Include CIDs in the story

APPENDIX D

TEMPLATE FOR DEMONSTRATION OF USER STORIES

Agenda:

- ✓ Clear and loud voice during the Demo, to understand the feature set.
- ✓ Communicate cancellation of meetings.
- ✓ Provide verification of screenshots and attachments for the user story being demonstrated.

Agenda:
Definition of Done Criteria (Criteria Met)

- ✓ Passed Unit Test.
- ✓ Passed Validation Test.
- ✓ Attached screenshot of the completed feature for verification purposes.
- ✓ Meets acceptance criteria defined in the User story.
- ✓ Demonstrated the completed feature successfully in the demo.
- ✓ User Story completion Approved by the BA.
- ✓ User Story completion accepted by the BA.
- ✓ Feature is ready and is shippable to the customer with zero defects.

Please join the below chatroom, for any issues.
GoTo://meeting/Resolution/us33678

APPENDIX E

SCRUM ENVELOPE: LIST OF USER STORIES READY

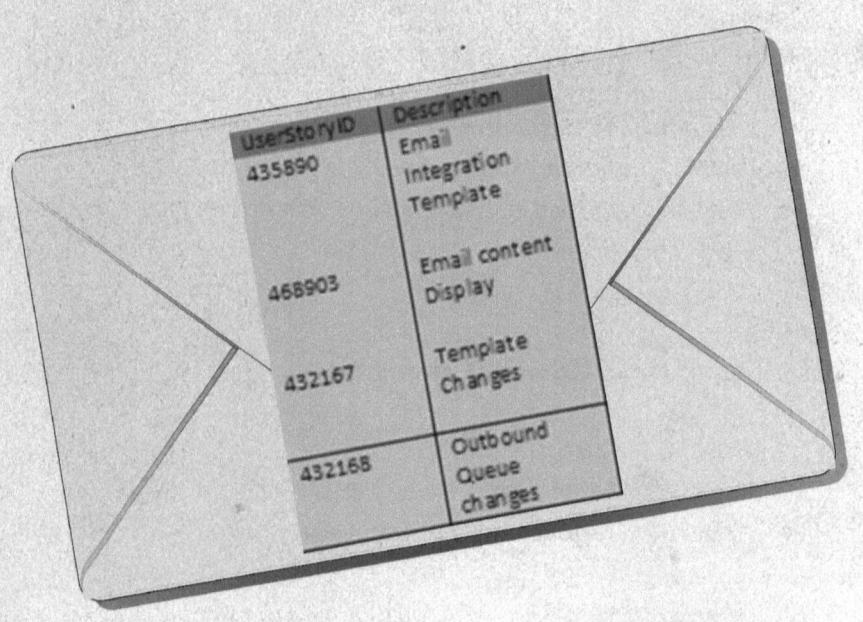

APPENDIX F

USER STORY TEMPLATE (TOOL)

- ✓ Title.
- ✓ Summary.
- ✓ Acceptance Criteria.
    - Includes (Technical Solution with proof of verification, includes HTML, CSS etc.).
- ✓ Release Date
- ✓ Project ID
- ✓ Developer assigned
- ✓ Task assignment
- ✓ Child user story
- ✓ Business Architect

User Story Readiness Requirement	Title of user story Summary of user story Technical Solution

APPENDIX G

TIMETABLE FOR DEMONSTRATION OF USER STORIES

✓ *Scheduling Demonstration of user stories drives efficient utilization of resources*

Id	Team	PO/POD	Demo Date	Demo Timeline
00654	MP	A	10/3/2017	9:30 am EST
00782	RA	B	10/4/2017	9:30 am EST
00276	HT	C	10/5/2017	8:30 PM IST
00215	GM	D	10/6/2017	9:30 am EST
00643	NK	E	10/9/2017	9:30 am EST
00785	MD	F	10/12/2017	10:00 am EST

APPENDIX H

USER STORY COMPONENTS

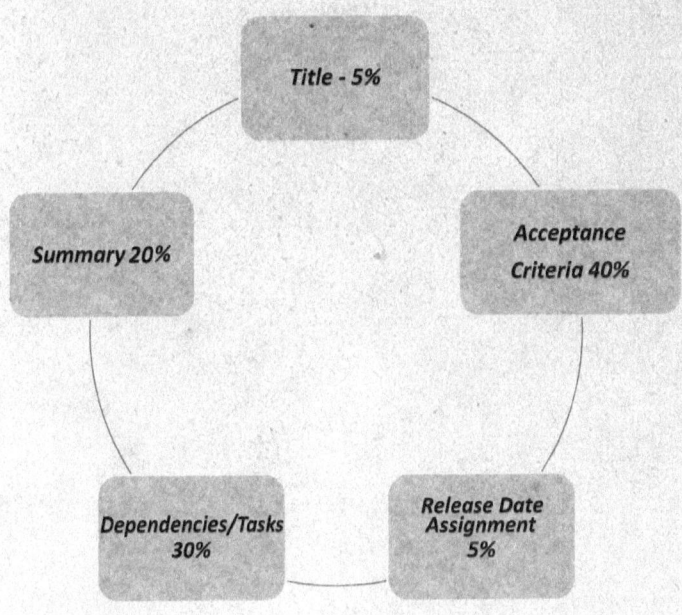

APPENDIX I

SCRUM SCRATCH PAD

First Unit
- Code/Development 15%
- Code Review 10%
- Unit Testing 15%
- Validation 15%

Second Unit
- Demonstration 10%
- Acceptance by Business Architect 5%
- Stakeholder Review 10%

Third Unit
- Stakeholder Acceptance 20%

APPENDIX J

SCRUM SCRATCH VALUE

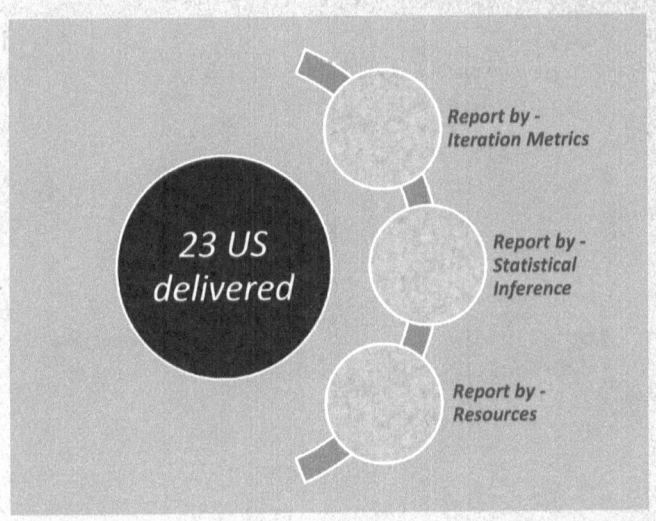

APPENDIX K

SCRUM SCRATCH CONTENT:

Number of user stories stories completed in an iteration → **Iteration score card**

↓

Iteration impact

↓

Iteration improvement cycles

↑

Improvement metrics

APPENDIX L

SCRUM CHAT CUBES

Facilitate project blockers and issues resolution through chat sessions/connect sessions.

Team identified below for Issues Resolution:

- ✓ Scrum Master
- ✓ BA/Architects
- ✓ Team members

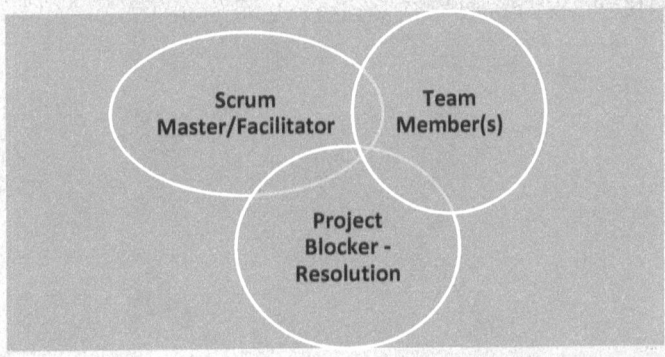

APPENDIX M

SCRUM SCRATCH PAD VALUE POINT ASSIGNMENT

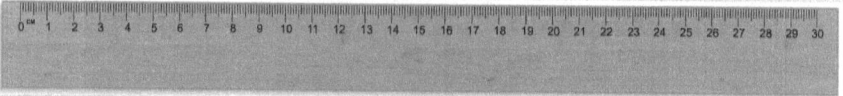

Scale of measurement – To measure Utilization (Consumption)

- 1 user story completed = 2 value points
- 1 defect = 1 negative value point
- 1 Readdressed user story = 1 negative value point
- 1 user story moved = 1 negative value point

APPENDIX N

SCRUM SCRUB PAD VALUE

- Scrum Scrub Pad Value: 41/50 * 100 = 82%
Delivered Stories – Defects addressed in the current iteration – Readdressed Stories (for partial fulfilment) – Moved Stories (Added late in the iteration and not addressed).

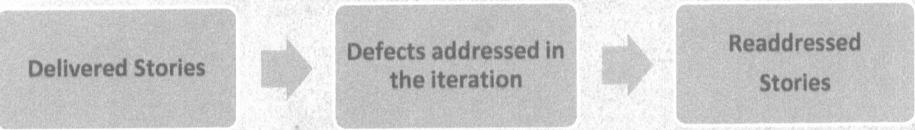

Note: Use value points (scale of measure)
Delivered stories = 25
Defects Addressed = 4
Readdressed user stories = 3
Moved stories = 2
Example:
*Percentage value = 41/50 * 100 = 82%*

Iteration1	Number	Value points
User Stories Delivered	25	50
Defects addressed	4	-4
Readdressed User Stories	3	-3
User stories Moved	2	-2
Total Value Points derived per iteration		**41**

APPENDIX O

SCRUM SCRATCH NOTE EXAMPLE

Scrum scratch note is an improvement comment and can be shown as a footnote in the Scrum Daily Report Pad.

> *Constraints in product fulfillment*

APPENDIX P

USER STORY COMPLETION TEMPLATE REPORT

User story linked to a completion template for reporting purposes can be standardized through a query and can be tagged for approval (Reference point for future planning)

Article:
Iteration number and user story number

Comprehension:
Screenshot verification
Code validated and reviewed
Test cases success scenarios

End Note:
Tagged and approved.

APPENDIX Q

ITERATION OPTIMAL VALUE POINT

Scrum Optimal Value Point is an average of 3 sequential iterations.

Optimal value point = 99.999% of user stories delivered

> Optimal Value Point = 99.999% of user stories delivered over 3 sequential iterations

APPENDIX R

SCRUM DAILY REPORT PAD (OPTIONAL)

Scrum daily report pad is useful for daily analysis/improvement scenarios, and a significant influential factor of metrics

Scrum Daily Report Pad
Scrum Header Note: *A significant indicator*
Scrum Table Data: *Task Progress factors*   − *Task progress factors of a user story.*
Scrum Footnote: *An improvement comment every day*

APPENDIX S

SCRUM RELEASE TIME TABLE EXAMPLE

Release Numbers mapped to Iteration Numbers

Release No's	Iteration Number
R6 07.06	Iteration 1
R7 08.06	Iteration 2
R8 09.07	Iteration 3
R9 10.19	Iteration 4

Release of an iteration can be broken down by the following categories
Bi-Weekly Release
Monthly Release
Quarterly Release
Annual Release

Example of Scrum Release Time Table
Weekly Releases: Defects/maintenance fixes
Monthly Releases: Iteration Releases
Annual release: IT Wide Release impacting all agile projects

APPENDIX T

SCRUM UMBRELLA

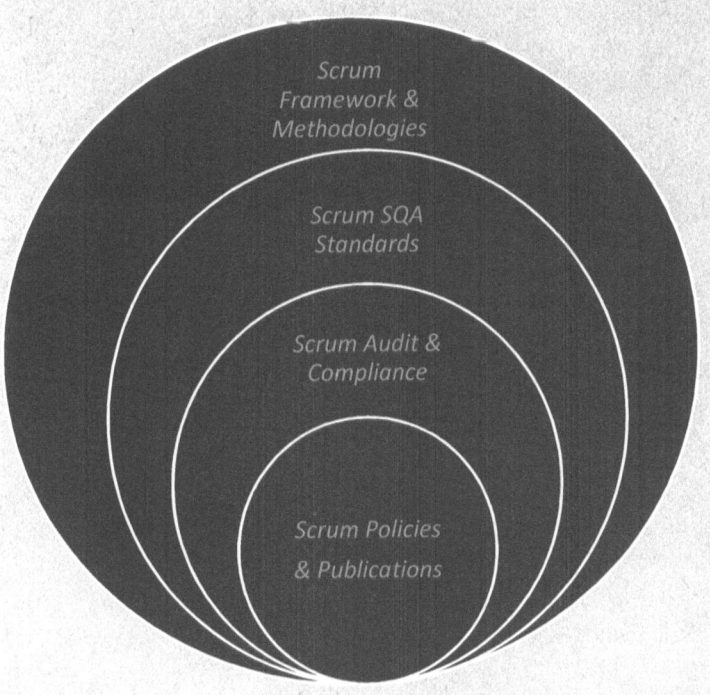

APPENDIX U

SCRUM TOOLKIT

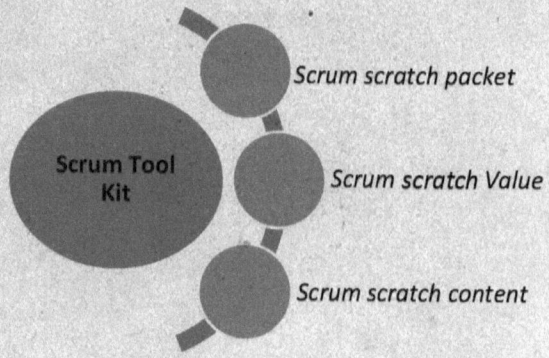

APPENDIX V

ITERATION SCORE CARD EXAMPLE

Category	Iteration1	Iteration2	Iteration3	Iteration4	Iteration5
xxxxxxxxxxx	xxxxxxxx	xxxxxxxx	xxxxxxxx	xxxxxxxx	xxxxxxxx
User Stories	20	30	35	36	40
Defects	5	4	4	3	2
Moved	5	3	4	4	2
Readdressed	4	2	3	4	2
Released stories	15	26	30	32	34
Accepted	13	23	28	30	33

APPENDIX W

MARGINAL UTILS CARD

Value points are computed using value added categories defined.

Value-Added Categories	Utils
Revenue value point increase over 2 iterations	>0 1 value point increase = 1 util (additional value derived).
Cost value point minimized over 2 iterations	Marginal reduced cost Compute utils (additional value derived).
Customer revenue increase: value point increase (Addition of customers)	>0 Compute utils (additional value derived).
Other factors that increase product value - **For categorization**	Need to be categorized to compute value.

www.ingramcontent.com/pod-product-compliance
Lightning Source LLC
Chambersburg PA
CBHW030913180526
45163CB00004B/1814